It was a small college, in wooded mountains, its students drawn from the impoverished Episcopal gentry of the South, its boarding-houses and dormitories presided over by widows of bishops and Confederate generals. Great Southern names were thick—Kirby-Smith, Elliott, Quintard, Polk, Gorgas, Shoup, Gailor. The only things it wasn't rich in were worldly goods, sociology, and science. A place to be hopelessly sentimental about and to unfit one for anything except the good life.

William Alexander Percy,
Lanterns on the Levee

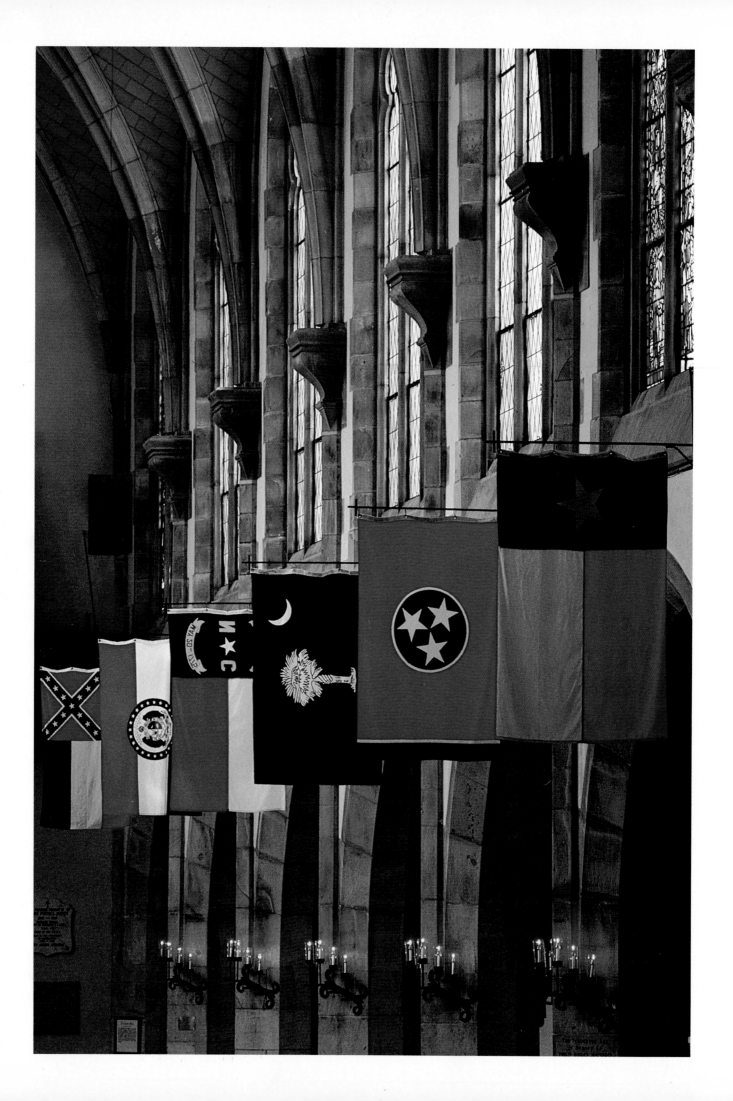

SEWANEE
The University of the South

Photography by William Strode

Harmony House
Publishers Louisville

Leonidas Polk

We deeply appreciate the help and enthusiastic support of The University of the South and Vice-Chancellor Robert Ayres, and, in particular, these people who contributed so greatly to the project: Beeler Brush, without whose guidance, and enthusiastic support this book would not have been possible; Mrs. Elizabeth N. Chitty; Mrs.Gertrude Mignery; and the Development and Alumni Office staff.

Executive Editors: William Butt and William Strode.
Library of Congress Catalog Number 84-082392
Hardcover International Standard Book Number 0-916509-01-X
Printed in Hong Kong by Everbest Printing Co. Ltd.
   for Four Colour Imports, Ltd., Louisville, Kentucky.
Third Edition printed in 1985 by Harmony House Publishers-Louisville
   P.O. Box 90, Prospect, Kentucky 40059.

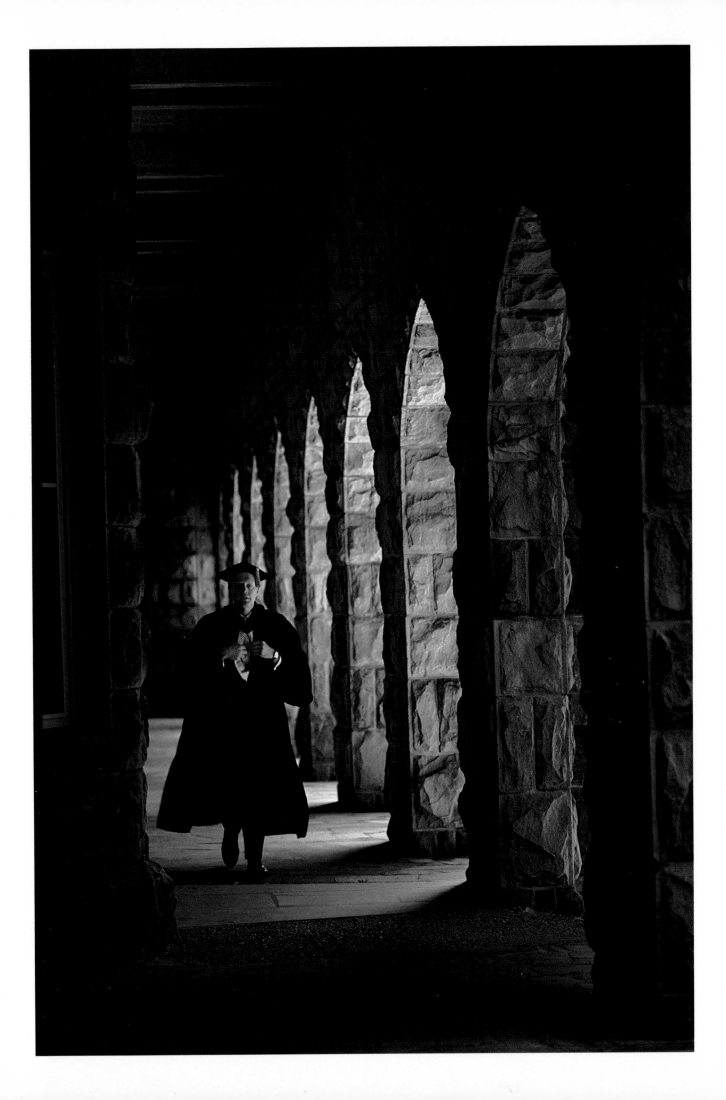

A CHRISTIAN UNIVERSITY AND THE WORD

by Andrew Lytle

WE ARE HERE TO BEAR WITNESS and perform an act of piety. We honor as we revive in memory those men who established this university, that our days may be long in the land. Only the very young can live in Eden. Only they can begin each day afresh, without memory, their senses quickening to the objects as they appear, as if they looked out upon the first day. This is a wonderful view, but it will not wear. Innocence prolonged ignores experience; knowledge denied becomes a stone in the head. Psychologists tell us that the state of innocence is the state we chiefly regret; and yet every man who is a man survives its loss; accepts the neccessity for knowledge and a responsibility for its use. But to do this you've got to know who you are, where you belong, and how to prosecute what talents God has given you.

Three bishops were our founders. Bishop Otey first had the idea; Bishop Polk gave it substance; Bishop Elliott became its image of learning and faith, the ideal made concrete in his person of what a Christian gentleman should be. Not that all three did not work in whatever way they could towards a common end, or that all three didn't share one another's virtues and courtesy. But it was Bishop Polk who finally made it happen. He studied universities at home and in Europe; he spread the need for a place of Christian learning; and he had persuasive gifts. He showed how in a short time of travel Sewanee could be reached from all the Southern dioceses; and by being maintained in common, the place would not strain beyond possibility any one community. The plan was good; it was unique almost. The university would begin, not haphazardly, but out of full knowledge of what a university should be, with a large endowment, not to be spent but whose interest would first raise buildings; then employ a faculty. Bishop Polk, having been a soldier, could distinguish between strategy and tactics. Since it would be founded to last, there was no need to rush in unprepared, at the mercy of improvised acts and decisions. The doors would open upon the full complement of teachers, halls, equipment, a library and of course a chapel. It was to be called the University of the South, a title as American as any, since the working parts of the Union have always been sectional. The university was expected to serve particularly the Southern dioceses, but it would open to all comers. A half

million dollars was quickly raised, the corner stone laid with thousands attending, coming by the trainload, by carriage, wagon, horseback and afoot. The South in all its parts, plain man, mountain man, planter, slave, man of affairs — all are here out of common respect for what was being done. The clergy and politicians spoke until the going down of the sun in praise of learning. This was October 1860.

In the spring of 1866 Sewanee was a wilderness again. The endowment gone, the few buildings burned down, the cornerstone blown up by enemy soldiers and carried away in their pockets as souvenirs. But they could not carry the land away, nor could they desecrate the idea for which the stone was laid. Men die and are defeated; an idea is eternal. In March 1866 Bishop Quintard with a few workmen entered this waste of trees, cut down a sapling and raised a cross twelve foot high, recited the creed, and sang Gloria in Excelsis. In this modest way the university was redeemed and rededicated.

This was the sign, and the hope, that nature and nature in man was once again to be reduced to order, without which no society can survive or its members live in worth and dignity. Off the mountain, in the valleys and plains there was another kind of waste. The South was beaten, exhausted, and tromped upon. Whole counties in Alabama and Mississippi didn't have even a needle. Houses burned, stock and cattle gone, some women pulled plows while men pushed to keep their children from starving. For ten years the ex-slaves led by carpetbaggers and scalawags combed the South for anything left by armies, levying taxes, bonding states for their private gain, selling counties of plantations under the hammer, dragooning and humiliating the defeated population. But still something remained, intangible, incomprehensible. The South was still undefeated in spirit. So the second war of conquest was set afoot, the conquest of the Southern mind. Francis Wayland, former president of Brown University, regarded the South as "a new missionary field for the national school teacher," and President Hill of Harvard looked forward to the job for the North of "spreading knowledge and culture over the regions that sat in darkness." These fellows figured they couldn't do the old soldiers much good. They would concentrate on the young and "treat them (the soldiers) as Western farmers do the stumps in their clearings, work around them and let them rot out."

Now, O venerable and brave,
The rock thou oft didst stand on (Darien
To th' unfoiled spirit of thee) we consecrate
In grateful reminiscence. Be thou still
Among us: soldier, father, friend;
Lover of all things fair,-trees, flowers, birds;
Ay, and God's creatures too,-the very snakes;
Intrepid, and therefore tender; stout and true;
A man of boisterous laughter and of stern
Command; of war if need be and of peace
To whoso peace ensueth. For thee we raise
The echoes that were wont to answer thee
In a free shout: Valiant spirit, all hail!
And may thy name and heart abide with us,
Sons of Sewanee, evermore! All hail!

Dr. William N. Guthrie

Kirby-Smith gravestone in cemetary

WELL, THERE WERE A LOT OF THOSE STUMPS at Sewanee in the form of Confederate generals and bishops, soldiers turned priests and priests who had been soldiers now turned teachers, and like walnut stumps it took a good deal of weather to rot them. They refused, like General Lee, to sell their names for fraudulent purposes; and with the sure instincts of an aristocracy, homespun though it may have been, turned to the true reconstruction of the South, the Christian education of their young men. It is very moving even now to read about these Cincinnati who once ruled in great affairs, living on short rations, in rough but beautiful surroundings, knowing however that the salvation of the South lay in the kind of thing they were doing. Out of the clear faith of a Christian view they knew that the Northern secular education relates to Christendom only in so far as it has for patron that old adversary, that fallen light which shines in darkness but does not illuminate. The lie we live today is that a secular society and a carnal world is the whole of life. It used to seem tedious to you gentlemen to come to chapel, but remember this. Only there could you feel yourselves belonging to a whole body, not just individuals engaged separately in a common end. I

have seen in a large land grant university (forbidden by law to hold religious services) the small buildings of various denominations lurking around the campus like houses of ill fame, which indeed they are to a secular court which has decreed prayer to be a criminal act. Ideas do have consequences and the perversion of ideas perverse conquences.

The South was a Christian society, but an incomplete one. It had as many puritans as New England. And they were fine people, but communion between Heaven and earth is bound to be uncertain, so long as you have only a pulpit and no sacrificial table before which to worship. Yet Southern people were believers as are all peole who are constantly at the mercy of nature and its laws. The seasons turn for a farmer (when there were farmers) and his welfare and even life depends upon this turning. The rough laws of nature may be defined, but nature is finally a mystery as it acts upon man. It is the very ground of a religious state of mind. When the formal religion of society knows less than the farmer about the mysteries of creation, then that society is likely not to know itself adequately and so suffer unneeded limitations. The great puritan heresy puts evil in the object, in a deck of cards, in a woman's hair, in dancing, in that great invention whiskey. The only time that church and state have got together in this country, since the Reformation, was to pass the prohibition law and create the most powerful and uncontrollable criminal class known in recent years. Evil cannot be in the object. It must be in the mind and heart. That's the only place it can be.

I'm not the one to say that the South would have been a more complete Christian society if the Episcopal church had been the only church. But it is true that under attack since the Missouri compromise, which frightened Jefferson like a firebell at night, all the sects were growing together towards one church. The South was struck down, unformed, before it knew itself. It had many diverse elements, but it had one institution which outlasted the destruction, which in this country and in Europe is the Christian unit, and that is the family. From the beginning here at the University the boys were put in boarding houses, so that they would have a home influence away from home. It was believed that without a woman's authority all manners would grow corrupt and all domestic virtues languish. The matrons in the dormitories are an extension of this and evidence of how an established practice must undergo outward change. As a basic part of society's structure the family has had to bear more than it ever was meant to. The recent attacks against the South are actually against the family, for so long as it thrives a dictatorship will have trouble. A family must have location that outlasts a generation. Family farms and plantations are becoming unprofitable; the families are breaking up and drifting away. The towns and cities are filling up with rabbit warren slums and carbon dioxide. No family, no human being can stand such a plight long.

Now what are we going to do to be saved? How can the university help? I feel that both the liberals and the conservatives have lost definition. Neither one can make us know what a liberal arts education means. But a tradition might. The essence of the Sewanee tradition has been that of the founders, to graduate a Christian or a gentleman, but preferably a Christian gentleman, who will go back home, or out into the world, and be what he is. That's the only way anybody can be of any use. First of all he will keep private things private and public things public. This is the basis of order. He will not speak of poetry to the philosophers or philosophy to the poets, as if he had all knowledge. If he wants to preach, then let him mount the pulpit; if he wants to influence politics, then let him run for office; if he wants to bring about social reforms, let him behave himself and mind his manners. His mind will presumably be a trained instrument which can respond to any kind of experience. He will let information go through him like a flux, but digest his learning. Some graduates will become scholars, but we will make a great mistake encouraging our best students all of them to go to graduate schools and perpetuate themselves. Now there are mixed and legitimate reasons for this; nevertheless it's the monkey going around the mulberry bush. There is another thing that at least wories me. It's not that television is going to supplant the flesh teacher. What worries me is all this instruction and fiats, from loans to examinations coming out of Princeton. If it keeps up we'll be writing up there to find out what textbooks they'll be pleased to let us teach, and we will get a reply from the moon.

Now I am going to wind up. In a society fast becoming proletarian, in an age that will become known as the paper age, is it possible to graduate Christian gentlemen, even from a school founded to deliver a Christian education? For make no mistake about it, this kind of education is aristocratic. It can't be democratic. We've never had a democracy in this country. We once had a Republic. Since the Civil War we've had a plutocracy. It calls itself a democracy, but then it is customary to betray in the name of what is being betrayed. The Union, for example, was destroyed in the name of defending it. How can a gentleman function and be himself in an ochlocracy, towards which we are moving?

THE IMAGE FOR A GENTLEMAN has been with us for a long time. It has survived from before the days when Christendom was rent. I think we have to go back to that. The world's plight is so precarious that we can not survive without a return to order and for us this can only be Christian order. Christendom was not a commonwealth; it was a god's wealth. The king was God's secular overseer; the bishop His spiritual. If you were the king's man, there was no doubt as to your place and degree, or likewise if you were the bishop's. Nobody mistook a man's function or place. The castle and cathedral stood forth for every eye to see, symbols both of physics and metaphysics. This entire order was held together, in the right order of relationship, by the Word, the eternal Word, for God said "Before Abraham was, I am," that is to say, I am pure being, pure creation, which is forever. The Word was God in His Creative function. There was God the Father, the lover, and God the Son, the beloved, and the Holy Spirit as the love which played between them. As the Holy Spirit this love came down from on high, in the likeness of a dove, to whisper into Her Ladyship the Virgin's ear the promise of salvation: to make flesh of the Word and the Wisdom that had created the flesh. Where else could the Word enter except by the ear, enter as the divine harmony of music, joining reason, imagination, the sensibility together to make the flesh to hold the spirit? Once before the dove brought to the ark a sign of reprieve. The doves were Aphrodite's attendants, symbolizing in their cooing her nature. Now at last with its fiery wings the dove as spirit entered invisibly matter, rendering not half man and half god but God incarnate. This is the mystery become the order Christians knew.

But this order fell (the world is much given to falling) and it fell first at the hands of priests, out of a lust for the total power of both rules; then Henry VIII usurped the authority which belonged to the lords spiritual. For both we can have but sympathy and charity, particularly for the priests who forgot the meaning of the sacrament and faltered as men. Ever since, the Word in Itself has gradually withdrawn into Itself, and the word as language without which man cannot know man nor get his business done has lost its divine form. Theology became partizan, but the divine glow was slow to leave language. The Spanish priests, not understanding that the imagination might be part of God's Word, spoke of Amadis de Gaul and Don Quixote as lying histories. Young soldiers too believed, which caused them to imitate Amadis and so hazard the lives of their friends who had to rescue them from heroic acts. The Word divine had become the word magical: this was the clear step away from meaning. After the sixteenth century decline was rapid. And now with few exceptions, the word is secular, legal, with no fixed definition. It serves to increase our appetites and to disguise the truth, and make us the slaves either to ourselves or other men. Whole forests are cut down daily towards this end. But there is hope. We were promised one thing: that the gates of Hell would not finally prevail. It is time to take the risk of judgement. A Christian university can begin to restore to language its meaning: first by definition which defines, makes more accurate the vocabulary of the various branches of learning, keeping them in their right order and relationships. This is the beginning of recovery, for without knowledge there can be no apprehension of the divine creative promise of the Word. There are words still with symbolic lustre, like sine and cosine, and honor.

Let us take the word honor, since it involves the whole action of man and not merely his profession. In Mississippi, Colonel Dabney, who had been a rich planter before the Civil War, afterwards found himself ruined. A white-haired old man, he did the family wash, because Sherman had said he would bring every Southern woman to the wash board. Also, in his prosperous days, in the routine of business, he had put his hand to a note, promising to pay. In the reversal of fortune, which any one of us might expect, he found his obligation increased a hundredfold. He paid every penny of it, working only for this, and then died. He did not bemoan the turn of fortune that made of a simple matter a heroic act. His name was on that note. It was the symbol to himself. It defined him, himself to himself and to others. That signature meant that he would deny himself, his total being, if the note remained unpaid. It also meant submission to another, so long as the promise to pay was not paid. To redeem his word was to make him free. About the same time Jim Fisk tried to corner gold. When he failed, he said, "Nothing lost save honor." So, gentlemen, you have your choice.

That statement is the core of Yankee triumph over the South and its European inheritance. It means nothing matters but money. A man who so believes makes of himself a slave to an abstraction, his wife a fancy woman, and his children orphans. How could there be so many divorces if this were not the case, or so many children lost?

The University of the South maintains at least the rumor of its founders' intentions. In that is a motie of hope: that it should turn out a Christian gentleman and today of necessity it must add gentlewoman, even though these words have become anachronistic. But the university still offers the disciplines of a Liberal Arts education, at least a sound education. We may take comfort in this.

The mountain and the past

Photographs for this section were chosen from the University's photographic archives under the supervision of Mrs. Gertrude F. Mignery. Copy photography and prints produced by Coulson Studio, Cowan, Tennessee. All text for these photographs was researched and written by Mrs. Elizabeth N. Chitty.

Rebel's Rest was built in the summer of 1866 by Major George R. Fairbanks and occupied until 1966 by his descendants. Here lived the first students, here the Board of Trustees in 1866 decided to revive the University, and here the faculty club, the EQB, was founded in 1870. It is now the University's guest house.

"Forensic Hall on the north side of (St. Augustine's) chapel, 60x36 feet, was erected largely through private aid, and was put up within the space of three weeks, much of the lumber used having been cut down, hauled to the mill, sawed and thence to the ground during the progress of the erection." Vice-Chancellor Josiah Gorgas to the Trustees, 1875. "Dear to the heart (of the summer girl) was old Forensic, built by the students in 1874, under the leadership of Caskie Harrison. A sun dial marks the spot where that rough unpainted building, with its wooden shutters and unglassed rose window, stood for 35 years, the center of social life at Sewanee . . . Old Forensic could have told many tales of beaux and belles, of Red Ribbon Germans, and Snake and Fox Head dances . . . Another Memory of Forensic was the Declamations and Debates, when every contestant received bouquets of garden flowers from his lady admirers." (Sarah Hodgson Torian in *Purple Sewanee*.)

This photograph with caption "Mass Meeting of Students 1889" came from the scrapbook of H.H. Edgerton.

The original Fulford Hall was completed in 1866 when Bishop Quintard and his family moved to University Place, as Sewanee was then known. The house burned in 1889 and was replaced by the present Fulford, which now has lost its Victorian turrets and towers. In one version or another, Fulford Hall, on this spot, has housed seven Vice-Chancellors.

Otey Hall was built in 1866 for a Tennessee diocesan seminary and then was given to the University. Here lived some of the first students in 1868 when the Junior Department opened with nine students and four professors. The house stood in front of the present Walsh Hall.

When Tremlett Hall was first occupied in 1869, students lived on the upper floor and the families of Col. T. Frank Sevier and Brigadier-General Josiah Gorgas on the first floor. The occupants ranged from Grammar School students in uniform to Gownsmen, who may have been senior students in the College or seminarians at St. Luke's across the park. Tremlett Hall was named for the British clergyman who arranged Bishop Quintard's 1867-68 fundraising tour which made possible the opening of the University and who received the University's first honorary degree. The hall stood just south of the present Kirby Smith monument.

"The road was new, very uneven, with sharp curves winding around the mountain side and a grade of 135 feet to the mile." (An 1850's description from the Sewanee Sampler.) The track from Cowan to the coal mines in Tracy City passed over a tunnel on the main line between Nashville and Chattanooga. Affectionately known as the Mountain Goat, at one time it had four passenger trains up the mountain each day, but even caboose service was abandoned when Amtrak came into being. An occasional freight train still uses the track.

Palmetto Hall, on St. Augustine's Avenue, "the biggest boarding house in Sewanee" according to young Ely Green in Too Black, Too White, was built in 1872 as one of three DuBose houses when the young chaplain moved to Sewanee from South Carolina.

"Magnolia—a name conjuring up visions of the dreamy Southland ... with wide piazzas and open-hearted hospitality....from such a background Moss Maria Porcher came to Sewanee, and gave the house she built in 1872 a name that would connect it, wistfully, with her native state of South Carolina. With orphaned nephews to educate...she cast her lot with the early days of the University. ...No one will ever know how many boys were taken in Magnolia for half-pay, or none at all, and given their chance for an education." (Purple Sewanee) Magnolia became the dining hall for the University and later faculty offices after the completion of Gailor Hall in 1952. It stood south of the present Woods Laboratories.

The Sewanee Grammar School was housed for nearly twenty years in the first of several structures known as "Sewanee Inn," or "The Hotel." The earlier part of the building on the left was constructed in 1869 by John D. Phelan, a former legislator, circuit judge, and member of the Alabama Supreme Court, who moved to Sewanee and took paying guests into his home, "The Forks," at the junction of University and Tennessee Avenues. The Grammar School moved from this site to Qunitard Hall, upon completion of that structure in 1902, a memorial to the first Vice-Chancellor and Bishop of Tennessee, Charles T. Quintard. In 1908 the Grammar School became Sewanee Military Academy, then Sewanee Academy, before its merger in 1981 with St. Andrew's School.

Quintard Hall, Sewanee Military Academy, before a fire in 1919 destroyed the interior. The massive stone building, rebuilt, served in turn the Sewanee Grammar School, the Sewanee Military Academy, and Sewanee Academy from its completion in 1902 until the merger of the school with St. Andrews School in 1981.

"A little before 5:00 crowds were seen collecting on the drill grounds . . . a motley mixture of grammar school students, theologues, ladies, professors, gownsmen and covites, to say nothing of the handsome cadets in their neatly fitting grey uniforms," (University of the South Magazine, August, 1890.) "From the Convocation Hall to the trees in Manigault Park was our drill ground, being also the Old Hardee Baseball grounds. Here we assembled at daylight's early dawning and drilled until breakfast time." (Purple Sewanee, about a somewhat earlier time, but the same locale.) In the background St. Luke's Hall, occupied in 1879. Manigault Park is named for the donor of St. Luke's, Charlotte Morris Manigault of Brighton, England, and South Carolina. St. Luke's Hall housed the School of Theology from 1879 until 1984.

"The finest seminary plant in America" when it was occupied in 1879, St. Luke's Hall was named by its donor, Mrs. Charlotte Morris Manigault of Brighton, England, and South Carolina, as a tribute to Bishop Charles T. Quintard of Tennessee, who had been a physician before entering the ministry. It housed the School of Theology from 1879 until 1984. The oldest permanent stone building, and the second erected for the University, the original interior of suites with fireplaces was entirely replaced in 1955.

When Manigault Park was landscaped about 1900, Major George R. Fairbanks said of the University Domain: "Its natural features, splendid forest growth, easily constructed avenues, its pellucid springs, gentle slopes, varied elevation and ravines present to the landscape gardener the opportunity of more extensive and beautiful elaboration than is possessed even at Biltmore, near Asheville, North Carolina." (Fairbanks, History of the University of the South.) In the background are St. Luke's Hall (left) and Breslin Tower and Convocation Hall (right). In the foreground are two gownsmen, senior students or perhaps faculty. Upperclassmen with good academic records have worn the academic gown to daily classes since 1871, but the cap has been largely abandoned.

"We drank Coca Colas in the Crow's Nest, which was built on the back of the old Supply Store." (Purple Sewanee, describing the 1890's at Sewanee.)

"Visitors complain very much about the cow monopoly in the question of street pedestrians. The first impression given to a stranger walking up University Avenue is that Sewanee is a large cattle ranch. This is a nuisance which should be abated." (Daily Purple, 1894.) Hence the fences.

Miss Johnnie Tucker, whose mother was matron at Palmetto and then at Tuckaway, was the staunchest supporter of Sewanee athletics. Here she helps celebrate the 50th anniversary of Sewanee football in 1941 with the traditional cheer.

Thompson Hall, named now for its principal donor, Jacob Thompson, was known as "Chemical and Philosophical Hall" when it was completed in 1883, the earliest surviving stone building of the College of Arts and Sciences. It was the site of the Medical Department from its opening in 1892 to its closing in 1909. More than 600 doctors were graduated between those years. The building was then used as a student union, with theatre upstairs and from the 1930's, a movie theatre in the annex. Gutted by fire in 1950 the building was reduced to a single story, and it is now the location of the Development Office.

Jacob Thompson served as Secretary of the Interior under President Buchanan and then directed Confederate spy operations in Canada during the Civil War.

"We recommend that the Board of Trustees receive for the University $10,000 in cash in full of said legacy rather than rely upon the possibilities of the ($100,000 in) telephone stock" bequeathed by Jacob Thompson to complete payment of this building. (Proceedings of the Board of Trustees, 1885.) In this 1940's photograph the building now known as Thompson Hall housed sandwich shop, student post office, a theatre for lectures and dramatics on the second floor, and an annex for movies in the rear. Rebuilt within the original walls after a fire in 1950, it now houses the Development Office and the movie theatre.

Convocation Hall was used as a gymnasium and convocation house from 1886 to 1902, when the library was moved from Walsh Hall and other places on the campus. There the library remained until 1965 when the Jessie Ball duPont Library was opened on Alabama Avenue. The Vice-Chancellor in announcing the move of the library in 1901 said the building should become "our memorial hall and Westminster Abbey." With its portraits and memorial plaques it has served that purpose for many years. It has now been restored as a lecture and concert hall. The bearded gentleman on the rear wall is Confederate General Edmund Kirby Smith who taught mathematics and botany at Sewanee from 1875 to 1893. He was the last full general of the Confederacy (one of eight) to surrender and the last to die.

Convocation Hall, completed in 1886, as the chapter house for a chapel projected for the adjoining site now occupied by Walsh Hall, is attached to Breslin Tower. Breslin is designed after Magdalen Tower at Magdalen College, Oxford. The tower contains a set of Westminster chimes with tones similar to those in London. Breslin Tower was named for a young girl, Lucy, whose early death was much mourned by her parents.

"The Gay Nineties were the heyday of the Summer Girl at Sewanee. She arrived for the 4th of July Hop and remained for Commencement in August." This group had climbed Breslin Tower.

St. Augustine's Chapel was opened on Sept. 18, 1868
when the first students marched in while the plasterer was
still completing work on the interior. It was expanded
many times, "like a Bedouin's tent," before it was replaced
by All Saints' Chapel in 1910.

All Saints' Chapel, begun in 1904, was brought to this
appearance in 1910. For the University's Centennial
observance it was completed in 1957-59 when the walls
were raised, the wooden roof replaced, the chancel
extended, the office wing added and the tower and narthex
erected.

A Plan for the Completion of the College Quadrangle of the University of the South
By Edward McCrady, Jr., modified from an earlier plan by Silas McBee.

The interior of All Saints' Chapel, circa 1920, with its wooden beams, Oertel paintings in the chancel and unplastered brick walls, was not completed until 1959. These beams now support the pavillions at Lake Cheston.

1. **Emerald - Hodgson Hospital**
2. **St. Lukes Hall**
3. **St. Augustine's Chapel**
4. **Thompson Hall**
5. **Convocation Hall**
6. **Walsh Hall**
7. **Carnegie Hall**
8. **Cleveland Memorial Hall**
9. **All Saints' Chapel**
10. **Guerry Hall**
11. **Snowden Forestry Building**
12. **DuPont Library**
13. **Woods Laboratories**
14. **Juhan Gymnasium**
15. **The Bishop's Common**
16. **Wiggins Music Building**
17. **Hoffman Hall**
18. **Elliott Hall**
19. **Cannon Hall**
20. **Johnson Hall**
21. **Tuckaway Inn**
22. **Gailor Hall**
23. **Hunter Hall**
24. **Cleveland Hall**
25. **Benedict Hall**
26. **McCrady Hall**
27. **Malon Courts Hall**
28. **Trezevant Hall**

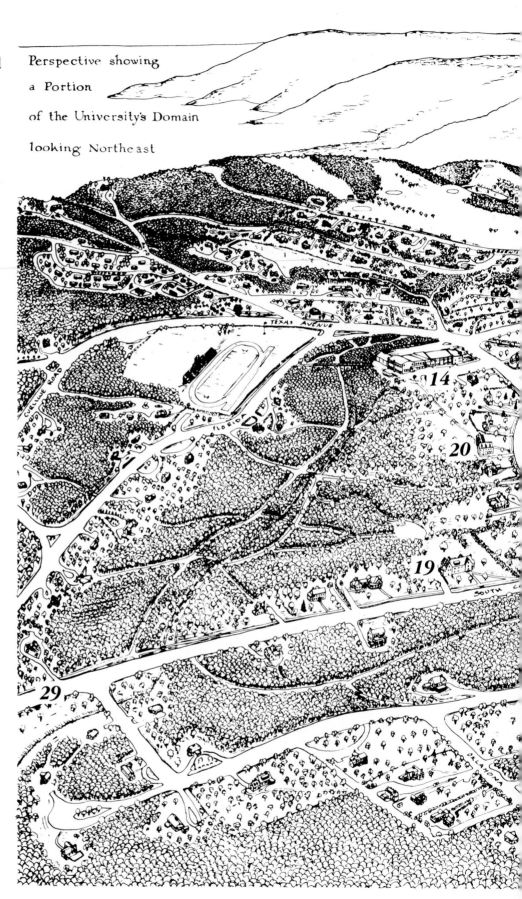

Perspective showing
a Portion
of the University's Domain
looking Northeast

THE COLLEGE OF ARTS AND SCIENCES OF
THE UNIVERSITY OF THE SOUTH
AT SEWANEE, TENNESSEE

The University

The Quadrangle. From left to right: Walsh Hall, built 1890; Cleveland Memorial Hall, 1965; Carnegie Hall, 1913; All Saints Chapel, 1905, 1957.

A towered city, set within a wood,
Far from the world, upon a mountain crest
There storms of life burst not, nor cares intrude,
There Learning dwells, and Peace is wisdom's guest.

Gardner L. Tucker

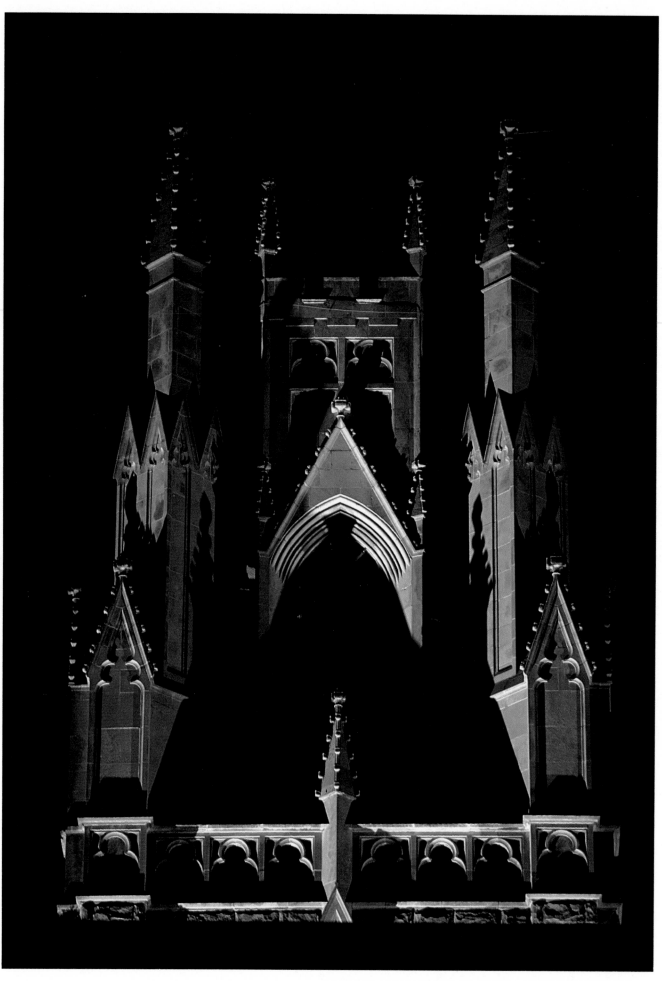

*Shapard Tower. It is 143 feet high and contains the 56-bell
Leonidas Polk Memorial Carillon, one of the largest in the world.*

The Rose Window

. . . this noble University of the South is evidence of this world-wide Anglican endeavor . . . I very much admire the pattern of education to be found here—a seminary at the heart of a thriving University and, at the heart of both, the chapel.

Robert A.K. Runcie, *Archbishop of Canterbury*, April 1981

The founding of the University, over the years, was a dedication to the faith of a great tradition. Actually, it is not difficult to define this faith. It is the faith that nature, reason and virtue are divine in origin and in sanction; that human life is ideally capable of attaining beauty and dignity; that the cultivation of knowledge, wit and good manners is a worthy human interest.

Dr. Charles T. Harrison, 1957

Elliott Hall

St. Luke's Hall. The first permanent building of the School of Theology, erected at the site of the University's ceremonial re-birth in 1866.

A window in Convocation Hall, built in 1886.

Top of Breslin Tower, modeled after Magdalen Tower, Oxford

Guerry Hall

Bust of Allen Tate in the DuPont Library.

The most that we can do with the past is to salvage what is good in the present and hold on to it; and that creates a new past.

Allen Tate, Founder's Day address, "A Trivial Meditation"

Sewanee has always been an intimate place in which close personal ties between the students themselves and the students and faculty could be developed. And in this intimate context Sewanee has always been interested in the whole man — his manners and morals as well as his information.

Dr. Edward McCrady, report to the Trustees, 1971

we are
outside
under a
tree

The founders from the first had a conception of this University as a place where the students should come in contact . . . with the best that has been thought and said in the world, and should do this in surroundings of natural and architectural beauty.

Lawrence F. Abbot, 1924

It is so beautiful that people who have once been there always, one way or another, come back. For such as can detect apple green in an evening sky, it is Arcadia.

William Alexander Percy,
Lanterns on the Levee

Malon Courts Hall

Gailor Hall

Lake Cheston

The emphases on good manners,
the coat and tie, the ladies in the
halls and at the dining tables are but
visible signs of the fact that Sewanee
has long considered itself a
repository for the hopes and dreams
of the Old South.

Arthur Ben Chitty, *A Brief*
History of The University of the
South

For a long time we were shut away here unheeded and unheeding. We liked ourselves, we enjoyed associating with ourselves; we were sorry for people who did not understand and appreciate Sewanee.

Sarah Barnwell Elliott, *Cap and Gown*, 1900

. . .And whatever the disadvantages of being off the beaten path, we here at Sewanee are still blessed with the capacity to personalize our relationships, to practice the art of living together, to learn how to grow in grace and in good manners.

Rt. Rev. Girault M. Jones, an address to the Trustees, 1979

Tuckaway Inn

Breslin Tower

*It is the aim . . . of The University
of the South to develop a harmonious
and symmetrical character, to fit and
prepare men for every avocation in
the life that now is . . . and to teach
all those things which a Christian
ought to know and believe to his
soul's health.*

Bishop Quintard, 1873, from an
untitled manuscript

St. Augustine's Chapel, in the sacristy wing of All Saints Chapel

*Present-day Sewanee, population
1500, is, depending on your point of
view, either a sleepy little Southern
town with a British accent or an
English village with a drawl.*

Alan Cheuse, *The New York
Times*, May 6, 1984

Site of the Sewanee Military Academy, new home of the School of Theology

Fulford Hall, traditional residence of the Vice-Chancellor

Walsh Hall

Green's View

And the stone and shingle house at Morgan's Steep,
built for Mr. Oertel, the painter,
is shipshape again, with a new roof and new floors—
near the site where John Hunt Morgan,
hotly pursued by Yankee cavalry,
galloped off the sandstone bluff
with important dispatches in his saddlebags
into the tops of black oaks and tulip poplars—:
an old story but not a true one,
we learn, after these years of telling it.

Richard Tillinghast, *Sewanee in Ruins*

Green's View

*Well, there is East, Middle, and West Tennessee, and there is also, say I, the Domain of the University of the South . . . And among these the bravest are the Domainians. This is so, in my opinion, because Sewanee has had the courage, certainly more than the other divisions of the state and more than any other college I know of, to insist upon retaining its own traditions, its own individuality, its own **particularities.** It has tried, as any institution which is to endure must, to make the world relevant to its own principles and ideals rather than to accept the values of the world.*

Peter Taylor, Founder's Day Speech, 1972

I believe in Sewanee with all my heart. I do not know of any institution of its size in any part of our country which has done more for the cause of good citizenship than Sewanee has done. As an American I am proud of it; as a citizen I am grateful to it. It is entitled THE UNIVERSITY OF THE SOUTH, but is much more than that; it is the University of all America, and its welfare should be dear to all Americans who are patriotic and farsighted, and therefore anxious to see every influence strengthened which tends for the betterment and enlightenment of our great common country.

President Theodore Roosevelt, 1907

IN MEMORY OF
EGBERT BARROWS FREYER 1902-19

1960

Charles A. Stair, Memphis.
Rev. Alfred Robert Taylor, San Diego, Cal.
Albert H. Waldon, Datona Beach, Fla.
Barbara Porter Ware, Sewanee.
Charles W. Waring, '20, Charleston, S.C.
George Bryant Wheelus, '57, Beaumont, Tex.
Kenneth G. Whitaker, Sr. '20, Chattanooga.
Silas Williams, '09, Chattanooga.
Dr. T. H. Williams, Chickasha, Okla.
Willie Six Sims, Sewanee.
Very Rev. Jas. Wilmer Gresham '35, San Francisco
J. H. Percy, Baton Rouge, La.
John Nicholas Lewis, Newport, Ark.
Victor Joseph Kutzweg, Placquemine, La.

Gifts have
been made
in memory
of the
persons
whose names are
inscribed in this Book.

"I come back to the mountain often and see, with a pang, however different it may be to me, it is no different . . . Then with humility I try to blend and merge the past and the present, to reach the unchanging essence."

William Alexander Percy,
Lanterns on the Levee